A Pillar Box Red Publication

in association with

THE BEST FOOTBALL MAGAZINE!

MATCH!
THE BEST FOOTBALL MAGAZINE!

FOOTBALL SKILLS

Written by Jared Tinslay & Jamie Evans

Edited by Stephen Fishlock

Designed by Darryl Tooth

TRICK KINGS!

The footy planet is packed with sick skillers! MATCH counts down the world's Top 50 – and rates their best tricks too! Check it out...

50 MOHAMED SALAH

Club: Liverpool
Country: Egypt
DOB: 15/06/92

The Liverpool winger is an expert at pulling off the inside chop – he tempts the defender one way, before busting out the epic skill move and then moving into the space he's created. That's how he gets so many shots off!

CONFIDENCE	DRIBBLING	TRICKS	AGILITY	WEAK FOOT
90	90	75	87	50

49 OUSSAMA ASSAIDI

Club: FC Twente
Country: Morocco
DOB: 15/08/88

The tricky Twente winger might have flopped in the Prem for Liverpool and Stoke, but he's got loads of jaw-dropping skills! He's got such quick feet that he can tie defenders in knots!

CONFIDENCE	DRIBBLING	TRICKS	AGILITY	WEAK FOOT
80	80	92	90	80

48
AMINE HARIT

Club: *Schalke*
Country: *Morocco*
DOB: *18/06/97*

Any player that's dubbed 'The Next Zinedine Zidane' must have sick ball control – and Harit definitely does! The Morocco midfielder is so elegant with the ball at his feet, and he can whip out the Zizou roulette with ease!

CONFIDENCE	DRIBBLING	TRICKS	AGILITY	WEAK FOOT
80	83	83	85	75

47
RICHARLISON

Club: *Everton*
Country: *Brazil*
DOB: *10/05/97*

Watch how the mega powerful Brazil winger waits for the defender to commit himself, before tapping the ball past him and using his jaw-dropping acceleration to drive into dangerous areas. Ledge!

CONFIDENCE	DRIBBLING	TRICKS	AGILITY	WEAK FOOT
85	80	75	82	95

46
JULIAN DRAXLER

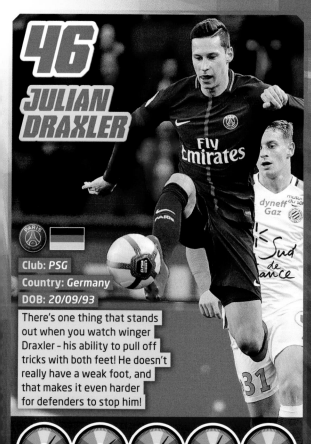

Club: *PSG*
Country: *Germany*
DOB: *20/09/93*

There's one thing that stands out when you watch winger Draxler - his ability to pull off tricks with both feet! He doesn't really have a weak foot, and that makes it even harder for defenders to stop him!

CONFIDENCE	DRIBBLING	TRICKS	AGILITY	WEAK FOOT
85	89	85	83	99

45
DELE ALLI

Club: *Tottenham*
Country: *England*
DOB: *11/04/96*

Is there a better player on the planet than Alli at pulling off a cheeky nutmeg? The confident Tottenham midfielder's nutmeg-to-game ratio must be insane! He's always trying out new tricks in matches, too!

CONFIDENCE	DRIBBLING	TRICKS	AGILITY	WEAK FOOT
90	88	88	80	78

44 RODRYGO

Club: *Santos*
Country: *Brazil*
DOB: *09/01/01*

You don't get named 'The Next Neymar' for just being Brazilian! The Samba forward, who'll join giants Real Madrid in 2019, already has a ton of skill compilation videos on YouTube, and he only turned 17 in 2018!

CONFIDENCE	DRIBBLING	TRICKS	AGILITY	WEAK FOOT
87	90	88	85	80

43 LEROY SANE

Club: *Man. City*
Country: *Germany*
DOB: *11/01/96*

Seeing speedster Sane running at you must be one of the scariest sights for a defender – especially when you know he can skin you so easily with a drop of the shoulder! The winger does it time and time again for City!

CONFIDENCE	DRIBBLING	TRICKS	AGILITY	WEAK FOOT
90	91	75	95	75

42 VITINHO

Club: *Flamengo*
Country: *Brazil*
DOB: *09/10/93*

Footy stars with names ending in 'inho' tend to be tricksters – and forward Vitinho is no different! The fact he can bust out a double-cut with either foot gains him a few positions on our shortlist, too!

CONFIDENCE	DRIBBLING	TRICKS	AGILITY	WEAK FOOT
90	83	92	80	100

41 DAVID NERES

Club: *Ajax*
Country: *Brazil*
DOB: *03/03/97*

Neres has been a real crowd-pleaser since joining the Eredivisie in 2017! The ace left-footed right winger loves cutting inside onto his stronger foot, and has incredible pace to break away from defenders too!

CONFIDENCE	DRIBBLING	TRICKS	AGILITY	WEAK FOOT
90	87	88	88	80

40

ROBERTO FIRMINO

Club: Liverpool
Country: Brazil
DOB: 02/10/91

The striker's signature skill has become the sick no-look goal – something which total Brazil legend Ronaldinho first brought to the game! MATCH reckons those sort of goals should be worth double in the scoring charts!

TOP SKILL!
NO-LOOK GOAL!

CONFIDENCE
90

DRIBBLING
80

TRICKS
85

AGILITY
87

WEAK FOOT
88

MATCH! ACADEMY
Play like the stars!

GABRIEL JESUS
SIDE STEP SCISSORS!

TIP 1: GAME USE

The Side Step Scissors is effective in a 2 v 1 situation as a fake outside foot pass to an overlapping team-mate, because it helps create space so you can travel with the ball in the opposite direction! Samba superstar Gabriel Jesus does it all the time when he links up with his lethal Brazil attacking team-mates!

TIP 2: DEFENDER POSITION

Use the Side Step Scissors 1 v 1 move when you have a defender blocking you right in front or just behind. Watch superstar striker Jesus doing it all the time in the Premier League for champs Man. City - it's one of the reasons he's so hard to defend against!

THIS SKILL HELPS YOU...

Create opportunities to shoot and pass! ✓

Become unpredictable to defend against! ✓

Combine with your team-mates! ✓

TRAINING GROUND!
Now practise the Side Step Scissors!

STEP 1

Step behind the ball with the outside of your right foot and dip your shoulder (side step).

STEP 2

As your right foot touches the ground, move the outside of your left foot around the ball (scissors).

STEP 3

Now, push the ball away to your right with your right foot and leave your marker choking on dust! Repeat using your left foot to side step/push away and your right foot to scissors.

NOW WATCH EPIC VIDEOS!

Learn how to do loads of top tricks by visiting the MATCH Academy section on our website!

www.matchfootball.co.uk

FIFA SKILLS

Try busting out some of these simple skills on EA Sports' FIFA!

DRAG BACK ★★

This is a really simple skill move to turn away from defenders!

HOLD: R1/RB + L Stick Down

BALL ROLL ★★

This lets you shift the ball from one side to the other. Easy!

HOLD:	OR HOLD:
R Stick Left	R Stick Right

STEPOVER ★★

This is a proper classic move to beat your opponent!

ROTATE: R Stick Up, Left

OR ROTATE: R Stick Up, Right

NO TOUCH ★

Keep your opponent guessing without touching the ball!

HOLD: R1/RB

TOP TIPS!

When you see an arrow pointing upwards, that means flick or hold the right or left stick the way that your player is facing, and the down arrow is behind you!

You don't have to learn every single trick off by heart. Master one or two first, then add the other skills to your arsenal one by one!

Go to player info to check out your players' skill rating. 5-star skillers can do every trick in the book, but 1-star skillers can only do the basics!

FAKE SHOT ★

Line up a shot, then pull out a dummy to go the other way!

TAP: Circle/B + Cross/A

39

ALEXIS SANCHEZ

TOP SKILL!
THE SLAP CUT!

Club: Man. United
Country: Chile
DOB: 19/12/88

There aren't many forwards on the planet with better close control than the Prem dribble king! He keeps himself really low to the ground, and then with small touches and bursts of speed, can scurry away from his opponent!

CONFIDENCE
95

DRIBBLING
93

TRICKS
80

AGILITY
93

WEAK FOOT
75

38

AIDEN MCGEADY

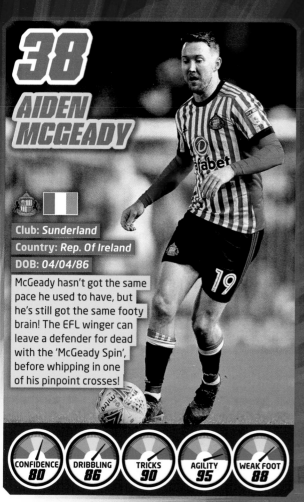

Club: Sunderland
Country: Rep. Of Ireland
DOB: 04/04/86

McGeady hasn't got the same pace he used to have, but he's still got the same footy brain! The EFL winger can leave a defender for dead with the 'McGeady Spin', before whipping in one of his pinpoint crosses!

CONFIDENCE 80	DRIBBLING 86	TRICKS 90	AGILITY 95	WEAK FOOT 88

37

FRANCK RIBERY

Club: Bayern Munich
Country: France
DOB: 07/04/83

The fact Ribery's in his mid-30s and still plays at the highest level proves how good he is! The winger's perfected some of the best tricks in the book, including the pull-push behind and reverse drag push!

CONFIDENCE 90	DRIBBLING 92	TRICKS 92	AGILITY 88	WEAK FOOT 80

36

EDEN HAZARD

Club: Chelsea
Country: Belgium
DOB: 07/01/91

The Belgium baller has got a low centre of gravity and epic agility. With his back to goal, the winger swivels away from defenders and leaves them choking on dust as he runs through on goal!

TOP SKILL!
CUT AND TURN!

CONFIDENCE 90	DRIBBLING 94	TRICKS 80	AGILITY 94	WEAK FOOT 88

35
MOHAMED ELYOUNOUSSI

Club: Southampton
Country: Norway
DOB: 04/08/94

Elyounoussi is definitely the stepover king! He once did 12 straight stepovers in a match back in 2013, before nutmegging his marker and skinning two men! A few years on, and now the forward is bossing the Prem!

| CONFIDENCE 85 | DRIBBLING 88 | TRICKS 95 | AGILITY 86 | WEAK FOOT 90 |

34
ISCO

Club: Real Madrid
Country: Spain
DOB: 21/04/92

Kids in Spain grow up playing futsal – the epic indoor footy game which is all about close control and fast-moving exchanges! That's why their midfielders are such technical wizards – and Isco's easily one of the best examples of it!

| CONFIDENCE 90 | DRIBBLING 90 | TRICKS 85 | AGILITY 83 | WEAK FOOT 80 |

33
VINCENT ABOUBAKAR

TOP SKILL!
THE ELASTICO!

Club: Porto
Country: Cameroon
DOB: 22/01/92

When the lethal striker isn't busting nets for his club and country, he's pulling off some worldy skills! We've seen him do loads of mind-blowing tricks like the Hocus Pocus, Elastico and Rabona. Sick!

| CONFIDENCE 88 | DRIBBLING 86 | TRICKS 95 | AGILITY 80 | WEAK FOOT 75 |

32 MARCELO

TOP SKILL!
THE SCISSORS!

Club: Real Madrid
Country: Brazil
DOB: 12/05/88

Defenders aren't normally known for their top tekkers, but Marcelo's definitely an exception! He pops up all the time on Real Madrid's social media feeds doing ridiculously cheeky tricks in training!

CONFIDENCE	DRIBBLING	TRICKS	AGILITY	WEAK FOOT
100	85	85	78	70

31 IGNACIO PIATTI

Club: Montreal Impact
Country: Argentina
DOB: 04/02/85

Piatti is definitely the most savage skiller in the MLS! The midfielder drives at defenders using both feet, and then fakes to shoot before skipping past his man and getting a real shot on goal. So deadly!

CONFIDENCE	DRIBBLING	TRICKS	AGILITY	WEAK FOOT
90	85	90	87	85

30 PAULO DYBALA

Club: Juventus
Country: Argentina
DOB: 15/11/93

Watching the Argentina ace is a bit like watching Lionel Messi - the way the ball sticks to his left foot as he weaves his way past his man. With constant small touches, the Juventus forward makes it really tough for defenders to time their tackle right!

CONFIDENCE	DRIBBLING	TRICKS	AGILITY	WEAK FOOT
90	90	85	91	75

BRAIN-BUSTER!

How well do you know some of footy's best tricksters?

1. True or False? Neymar's dad was a professional goalkeeper who played for Brazil!

2. Which country did Ousmane Dembele score his first ever France goal against – England or Wales?

3. What year did Brazil baller Willian join Prem giants Chelsea?

4. Did Cristiano Ronaldo win more domestic league titles for Real Madrid or Man. United?

5. Name the French club that sick Belgium winger Eden Hazard made his senior debut for!

6. How many games did Wilfried Zaha play for Man. United – more than ten or fewer than ten?

7. Which African country does jaw-dropping dribbler Yannick Bolasie star for?

8. Which El Clasico team has Ricardo Quaresma played for – Barcelona or Real Madrid?

9. Which mega boot brand does Andriy Yarmolenko wear – Nike, adidas, Puma or New Balance?

10. Is Algeria flair king Riyad Mahrez left or right footed?

1 ....
2 ....
3 ....
4 ....
5 ....
6 ....
7 ....
8 ....
9 ....
10 ....

FACE IN THE CROWD

Can you spot ten jaw-dropping skillers in this pic? The stars below are all there somewhere!

Thiago Alcantara

Kylian Mbappe

Sofiane Boufal

Gabriel Jesus

Aiden McGeady

Richarlison

Dele Alli

James Rodriguez

Douglas Costa

Charly Musonda

ANSWER ON P6

FIFA SKILLS

You'll tie defenders in knots with these awesome FIFA skill moves!

CRUYFF TURN ★

Change direction with this top move and leave your opponent for dead!

TAP: Square/X /

THEN: Cross/A /

& FLICK: L Stick Down

CHOP ★★★

Use the inside of your boot to change direction mega quickly!

HOLD: L2/LT

TAP: Square/X + Cross/A

FLICK: L Stick Left or L Stick Right

ROULETTE ★★★

Bring back Zinedine Zidane's world-famous spinning skill move!

ROTATE:
R Stick Down, Rotate
270° through Left to Right

OR ROTATE:
R Stick Down, Rotate
270° through Right to Left

ELASTICO ★★★★★

Whip the ball from the inside of your foot to the outside like a legend!

ROTATE:
R Stick Right, Rotate 180°
through Bottom to Left

OR ROTATE:
R Stick Left, Rotate 180°
through Bottom to Right

BALL ROLL CUT ★★★★

Add extra flair to the basic move!

HOLD: R Stick Left,
then R Stick Right

OR: R Stick Right,
then R Stick Left

29 PAUL POGBA

Club: Man. United
Country: France
DOB: 15/03/93

Pogba's role in midfield is all about keeping the ball flowing, but fans see glimpses of his magic when the game gets crowded in the middle of the park. He'll often use a stepover to move himself into space, or pirouette past an opponent!

CONFIDENCE 100	DRIBBLING 92	TRICKS 90	AGILITY 75	WEAK FOOT 85

28 GELSON MARTINS

Club: Atletico Madrid
Country: Portugal
DOB: 11/05/95

What do you get when you mix frightening pace with sick tricks? A world-class winger capable of destroying any defence - just like Portugal young gun Martins. This guy will only get better, too!

CONFIDENCE 90	DRIBBLING 83	TRICKS 95	AGILITY 82	WEAK FOOT 75

27 JAMES RODRIGUEZ

Club: Bayern Munich
Country: Colombia
DOB: 12/07/91

The attacking midfielder has rediscovered his best form at Bayern and he's proving what a class player he is! His close control, technique and vision are absolutely out of this world!

TOP SKILL!
STEP-OVER SCISSORS!

CONFIDENCE 90	DRIBBLING 85	TRICKS 88	AGILITY 89	WEAK FOOT 80

26

LORENZO INSIGNE

Club: *Napoli*
Country: *Italy*
DOB: 04/06/91

In Italy, Insigne is known as 'The Magnificent One', and that's mainly down to his epic ball-playing abilities! The forward dances past defenders and has one of the best first touches MATCH has ever seen!

CONFIDENCE	DRIBBLING	TRICKS	AGILITY	WEAK FOOT
90	90	85	100	75

25

KINGSLEY COMAN

Club: *Bayern Munich*
Country: *France*
DOB: 13/06/96

We've seen the electric winger sit opponents down on their backsides with his epic pace and skills! He'll knock the ball past his man, speed past them and then cut inside towards the goal!

CONFIDENCE	DRIBBLING	TRICKS	AGILITY	WEAK FOOT
92	90	85	90	75

24

HATEM BEN'ARFA

Club: *Free Agent*
Country: *France*
DOB: 07/03/87

If you looked up the definition of 'showboater' in a football dictionary, you'd probably find Ben Arfa's name! Not all of the winger's tricks come off, but when they do, they look absolutely spectacular!

CONFIDENCE	DRIBBLING	TRICKS	AGILITY	WEAK FOOT
80	90	90	80	85

23
ANDRIY YARMOLENKO

Club: West Ham
Country: Ukraine
DOB: 23/10/89

The wicked left winger has a wand of a left foot – he can make magic happen with just one flick! Andriy's the master of the backheel pass and pull Cruyff flick – we've even seen him assist goals using them!

CONFIDENCE	DRIBBLING	TRICKS	AGILITY	WEAK FOOT
90	92	95	81	65

22
CHARLY MUSONDA

Club: Vitesse
Country: Belgium
DOB: 15/10/96

The tricky winger, who's on loan at Vitesse from Chelsea, is full of swagger! Instead of trapping the ball on the wing, he'll drop his shoulder and let it roll past him, leaving the onrushing defender for dead. Skills!

CONFIDENCE	DRIBBLING	TRICKS	AGILITY	WEAK FOOT
85	85	95	90	100

21
MARLOS

Club: Shakhtar Donetsk
Country: Ukraine
DOB: 07/06/88

Our fave Marlos moment ever was when the winger skinned three players before being brought down in the box – and then netting the penalty in sick Panenka style. Total skiller!

TOP SKILL!
SUPER QUICK BALL ROLLS!

CONFIDENCE	DRIBBLING	TRICKS	AGILITY	WEAK FOOT
90	87	95	92	80

20
GABRIEL JESUS

Club: Man. City
Country: Brazil
DOB: 03/04/97

The wicked City striker grew up playing street football in Brazil, and he was given the nickname 'Easy-Peasy' because really tough tricks were so simple for him! Now he's whipping them out in the Prem!

TOP SKILL!
BALL ROLL CUT!

CONFIDENCE 90

DRIBBLING 90

TRICKS 85

AGILITY 93

WEAK FOOT 80

MATCH! ACADEMY
Play like the stars!

LIONEL MESSI
DRAG SCISSORS!

TIP 1: GAME USE

Use the Drag Scissors 1 v 1 move as you head towards goal to create space for a shot with your right or left foot. Anytime you watch Barcelona, you'll see footy legend Lionel Messi using this mind-blowing skill to bamboozle defenders!

POWERED BY

COACHING

THE WORLD'S
NO.1
SOCCER SKILLS
TEACHING METHOD

WWW.COERVER.CO.UK

THIS SKILL HELPS YOU...

Create space to score more goals! ✓

Boss your opponent in a 1 v 1! ✓

Create more assists for your team-mates! ✓

TIP 2: DEFENDER POSITION

The Drag Scissors is the perfect 1 v 1 move to use when you have a defender blocking you right in front of goal. It helps create space and time to move either side of your opponent to have a shot – Messi absolutely loves it!

IN ASSOCIATION WITH...

adidas | coerver COACHING

 @COERVEREW

TRAINING GROUND!
Now practise the Drag Scissors!

STEP 1

Drag the ball with the inside of your right foot and, at the same time, hop in that direction (drag).

STEP 2

As your hopping foot lands, move the outside of your right foot around the ball (scissors).

STEP 3

Now, use the outside of your left foot to push the ball and accelerate away! Repeat using your left foot to drag/scissor and right foot to push away.

NOW WATCH EPIC VIDEOS!

Learn how to do loads of top tricks by visiting the MATCH Academy section on our website!

www.matchfootball.co.uk

WORDSEARCH

Can you find the names of these 30 legendary trick kings?

```
K A A E                                                                T W W M
Q K Z C                                                                V H W H
D H F J                                                                S E R R
C E I D                                                                U Y Z C
L N M I                                                                K B K C

I R F P I N W F E W K Q B G Z E B E Z W Q P L Z I F H D R Z
C Y T J Q K G F G R I P F N W L M U M Q J D T K U P E C U I
D I X V D O H I C K R B T P F U F O D A X W D I E G O Q Z D
E M S R Y L N Z Z O R P T E N S L S T Z T E Q C U Q H X N A
U H E U S O U D I N B Y C S W D O N F B W P M F I V I Z E N
T D F Z L F B B E D D E P A H E G V Q A Q O I N A C I D Y E
Z P M A K G R E B C P M B E Z W S K N G M X G B F F Y U R C
Q G A E W E N Q H C O O G O G J T I U G X I F T S Y S O U G
Y T F M F I G O C Y O Y S K Q I W U A I T H F A W T U R U X
R A F L Q N D T A V U Q A O M B B W Z O H K P A U I I W R U
H N D E Z G S G C P X A Z C W Z V C N T S J L M O V W H R Y
L O N U B F Y C N U V T K H I T Y G C H D L O M A P Z N W N
K D G Q L E F M M W Q X E A V Y C L H A I N N L T Z E L A D
O A L I B K J T S N Z J R F V D O R K R W M D E Y S L M E E
Y R V R L E R K O E D E L A Y V Z A P F I O X T A U N H V F
K A H Z G W E S E L L J O D G P K S P B C M V I L U W S V G
Q M A F P G L H W O A R N V Y N A U O G A J H S B E S T V C
Q I Y Z S I H I M C V G L N T N G L R Y B K S S V B V Z T G
X G D S N E A H K M O W X G V I F R V C X W P I L C H S U F
I X P E I B L P E D J C S V K B O B L E T G M E W L M E D R
R L D S A Q R O F C R G P S K M G V W O G R C R D T W I N W
F O G X M T J O O O V X E Y A A V G Y A Y R N B X R W S U W
U H Z E E Q J W P A O D E R R S W F T P P L D E V O V H A K
P V Z F C A M B M X S U I R R B W W I L B S S I C N S K B C
J U Z B H S G T P U G O I D J N X Z V R P N D H F A J X P H
J B N C C C Z J C Q E N M H E K W R B U C J Y U D L H O O R
Z J B W S A B N M H C Z A T H Q O R C L A O K T E D E Z M M
X S Q E U P L G O H Z Q Z F R N I O D Y N H X Z Y I I D S Q
I P P X I N F U A C U I L K A Y B B J Y T N H J N N O C I O
B P E U Q Q D N A U U T M L P J J I Q X O I V K W H N U G R
S C L W A H E Z W Z V W D Z O T M N H O N N M H R O G W M W
P A E U N V S N L R F O U S G M G H M V A U U K Q Q X M Y K
T N A T P V L G D T O V W K D D D O E J X J C U X G S H L W
X F J W E J X D J O J U D V F N N I O I B R A H I M O V I C
N I M T Y H A F N P I R Y Y P F S F F P Q V G M I T P Y K M
```

Asprilla	**Cruyff**	**Ginola**	**Le Tissier**	**Robinho**
Baggio	**Deco**	**Henry**	**Maradona**	**Romario**
Bergkamp	**Denilson**	**Ibrahimovic**	**Okocha**	**Ronaldinho**
Best	**Di Canio**	**Juninho**	**Pele**	**Ronaldo**
Cantona	**Figo**	**Kaka**	**Riquelme**	**Zidane**
Cole	**Garrincha**	**Kerlon**	**Rivaldo**	**Zola**

FOOTY MIS-MATCH

Study these snaps of Neymar skinning a defender, then find ten differences between them!

ANSWERS ON P60

TOP SKILL!
ONE FOOT SPIN!

19
WILLIAN

Club: *Chelsea*
Country: *Brazil*
DOB: *09/08/88*

The Brazilian winger's footy idol has always been legendary trick machine Ronaldinho! He tries to copy his style of play and the idea that you have to be happy on the pitch – and what better way than cruising past your opponent at top speed!

CONFIDENCE
90

DRIBBLING
88

TRICKS
88

AGILITY
90

WEAK FOOT
88

18 PHILIPPE COUTINHO

Club: Barcelona
Country: Brazil
DOB: 12/06/92

Coutinho is such an intelligent player – on and off the ball! Watch him – the CAM's always moving, and when he gets the ball, he'll constantly be looking up searching for areas to bust out a skill!

TOP SKILL! STEPOVER DUMMY!

CONFIDENCE	DRIBBLING	TRICKS	AGILITY	WEAK FOOT
90	90	88	95	88

17 YANNICK BOLASIE

Club: Aston Villa
Country: DR Congo
DOB: 24/05/89

You've got to be pretty special to get one of the five-star tricks named after you in FIFA! The 'Bolasie Flick' and shot looks so wicked when you pull it off on FIFA, but it looks even better when the wing wizard does it in real life!

CONFIDENCE	DRIBBLING	TRICKS	AGILITY	WEAK FOOT
85	90	95	85	85

16 SOFIANE BOUFAL

Club: Celta Vigo
Country: Morocco
DOB: 17/09/93

Boufal's epic solo Goal Of The Season contender for Southampton v West Brom in 2017 is what he's all about! The CAM picked up the ball in his own half, dribbled past five men and then placed his finish into the bottom corner. Class!

CONFIDENCE	DRIBBLING	TRICKS	AGILITY	WEAK FOOT
90	87	93	90	88

15 THIAGO

Club: Bayern Munich
Country: Spain
DOB: 11/04/91

With Brazilian parents and growing up in Spain, Thiago was always going to be full of flair! He's the planet's most daring CM, always looking to move forward with the ball using bold, mazy runs!

CONFIDENCE	DRIBBLING	TRICKS	AGILITY	WEAK FOOT
90	90	95	90	75

14 NANI

Club: Sporting
Country: Portugal
DOB: 17/11/86

Nani doesn't have the same rapid acceleration as the 21-year-old winger who tore it up at Man. United, but he still has quick enough feet to whip out a double stepover and completely fool a defender. Ledge!

CONFIDENCE	DRIBBLING	TRICKS	AGILITY	WEAK FOOT
90	87	95	92	90

13 KYLIAN MBAPPE

Club: PSG
Country: France
DOB: 20/12/98

The sick forward pulled off the perfect Sombrero against Caen in April 2018, then busted out loads more tekkers at the World Cup in Russia! He has the potential to become the world's No.1 skiller in the next few years!

CONFIDENCE	DRIBBLING	TRICKS	AGILITY	WEAK FOOT
90	95	85	90	85

TOP SKILL!
FAKE RABONA!

12
OUSMANE DEMBELE

Club: *Barcelona*
Country: *France*
DOB: 15/05/97

Barça bought Dembele to replace Neymar, and the France forward defo has similar swagger! Check out his goal v Villarreal last season - the epic chipped finish over the goalkeeper was pure class!

CONFIDENCE	DRIBBLING	TRICKS	AGILITY	WEAK FOOT
90	90	95	90	90

11
STEPHAN EL SHAARAWY

Club: *Roma*
Country: *Italy*
DOB: 27/10/92

The nifty dribbler introduced himself to Roma fans in the best possible way back in 2015 - scoring with a backheel goal! That was a sign of things to come, with the forward doing jaw-dropping tricks every week!

CONFIDENCE	DRIBBLING	TRICKS	AGILITY	WEAK FOOT
95	90	95	90	65

10
ANGEL DI MARIA

Club: *PSG*
Country: *Argentina*
DOB: 14/02/88

The winger was born on Valentine's Day, and what he loves most is making defenders blush! The master of the High Wave totally confuses defenders when he pretends to stop, but dashes on in the same direction!

CONFIDENCE	DRIBBLING	TRICKS	AGILITY	WEAK FOOT
95	86	95	92	65

FIFA SKILLS

How many of these silky skill moves can you pull off on FIFA?

STOP & TURN ★★★★

Protect the ball from the defender before quickly changing direction!

FLICK: R Stick Up, R Stick Left

OR: R Stick Up, R Stick Right

BALL ROLLS ★★★★★

This 5-star skill move is well easy!

HOLD: R Stick Down

ONE FOOT SPIN

Turn away from defenders in style!

FLICK: R Stick Down, R Stick Left   **OR:** R Stick Down, R Stick Right

HEEL-TO-HEEL FLICK
★★★★

Get this move right and defenders won't stand a chance against you!

FLICK: R Stick Up, R Stick Down

RAINBOW ★★★★

Flick the ball over yours and your opponent's heads. Top tekkers!

FLICK: R Stick Down, R Stick Up, R Stick Up

PAULO DYBALA
INSIDE TWIST-OFF!

TIP 1: GAME USE

Use the Inside Twist-Off 1 v 1 move as you're travelling across the pitch, looking to create space to run with the ball, shoot or play a killer through pass to a team-mate! Juventus and Argentina superstar Paulo Dybala is a proper expert at this wicked skill!

Paulo Dybala wears adidas® Glitch boots. To find out more, head to adidas.co.uk/glitch

THIS SKILL HELPS YOU...

Protect the ball! ✓

Make space to switch play! ✓

Create chances for yourself and your team-mates! ✓

TIP 2: DEFENDER POSITION

You should bust out the Inside Twist-Off 1 v 1 move when you have a defender blocking you in front or at an angle. Trick machine Dybala does it loads for club and country, which is why he bags so many goals and assists. What a total legend!

TRAINING GROUND!

Now practise the Inside Twist-Off!

STEP 1

Start off by pushing the ball diagonally forward with your left foot.

STEP 2

Now, use the inside of your right foot to cut the ball and twist-off diagonally.

STEP 3

Then use the same foot to burn away from the defender! Repeat using your left foot to twist-off and accelerate away.

NOW WATCH EPIC VIDEOS!

Learn how to do loads of top tricks by visiting the MATCH Academy section on our website!

www.matchfootball.co.uk

9

LIONEL MESSI

Club: *Barcelona*

Country: *Argentina*

DOB: *24/06/87*

Leo isn't really known for flash tricks, but the way he dribbles past defenders at ease is second to none! We reckon the forward's classy adidas Nemeziz boots must have some magnets in them!

TOP SKILL!

THE DRAG PUSH!

CONFIDENCE
100

DRIBBLING
100

TRICKS
85

AGILITY
92

WEAK FOOT
85

8
CRISTIANO RONALDO

Club: Juventus
Country: Portugal
DOB: 05/02/85

These days CR7 tends to do less skilling and more goals, but the hitman's still more than capable of producing stunning tekkers – his CL overhead kick in 2017-18 was proof of that! He still loves a stepover, too!

CONFIDENCE	DRIBBLING	TRICKS	AGILITY	WEAK FOOT
100	90	95	85	86

7
DIMITRI PAYET

Club: Marseille
Country: France
DOB: 29/03/87

You just have to watch CAM Payet curl in a worldy free-kick to see that he's got one of the sweetest techniques around! He even injured a goalkeeper with a classy feint shot back in January 2018. Mad!

CONFIDENCE	DRIBBLING	TRICKS	AGILITY	WEAK FOOT
100	90	90	85	90

6

JUAN CUADRADO

Club: Juventus
Country: Colombia
DOB: 26/05/88

It's no wonder Juventus have one of the best defences on the planet - they have to train against trick machine Cuadrado every day! The Colombian winger is probably the master of one-on-ones!

CONFIDENCE	DRIBBLING	TRICKS	AGILITY	WEAK FOOT
95	95	95	91	80

TOP SKILL!
THE DOUBLE SIDE-STEP!

5

WILFRIED ZAHA

TOP SKILL!
THE ROLL-TOP AND CHOP!

Club: Crystal Palace
Country: Ivory Coast
DOB: 10/11/92

In an interview with MATCH in 2018, Gary Cahill called Zaha the most skilful player in the world - and we don't think he's far off! The proper unpredictable forward can perform almost every trick in the book, which means he can skill himself out of any situation!

CONFIDENCE	DRIBBLING	TRICKS	AGILITY	WEAK FOOT
92	92	95	95	80

4
RICARDO QUARESMA

Club: *Besiktas*
Country: *Portugal*
DOB: *26/09/83*

Quaresma is so inventive that instead of using his weaker left foot, he came up with a new skill move - the Trivela! The way he shoots and passes with the outside of his boot is incredible - as he proved with his goal at the World Cup - and his heel touch against Osmanlispor last season was just unbelievable!

TOP SKILL!
THE TRIVELA!

DID YOU KNOW?
IN HIS 18-YEAR CAREER, THE WINGER HAS PLAYED FOR SEVEN DIFFERENT CLUBS IN SIX DIFFERENT COUNTRIES!

CONFIDENCE **95**

DRIBBLING **90**

TRICKS **95**

AGILITY **92**

WEAK FOOT **85**

CROSSWORD

Use these clues to fill in MATCH's tricky crossword!

ACROSS

2. African country where Norway hero Mohamed Elyounoussi was born! (7)

6. Shirt number Cameroon striker Vincent Aboubakar wears for Porto! (4)

7. Month that lightning quick Man. City winger Leroy Sane was born! (7)

9. Shirt number Marcelo wears for Real Madrid! (6)

13. Country where Ignacio Piatti's side Montreal Impact are found! (6)

15. Team Mousa Dembele joined Tottenham from! (6)

16. Nickname Liverpool fans call their goal king Roberto Firmino! (5)

17. Sick boot brand Brazil and Barcelona's Philippe Coutinho wears! (4)

18. Number of seasons Angel Di Maria spent at Man. United! (3)

19. Spanish team Alexis Sanchez has played for! (9)

DOWN

1. Number of league goals David Neres scored for Ajax in 2017-18! (8)

3. Stephan El Shaarawy's strongest foot! (5)

4. Lionel Messi's middle name! Clue... Iniesta! (6)

5. Number of league assists Dimitri Payet bagged in 2017-18! (8)

8. The country Isco scored his first Spain hat-trick against in March 2018! (9)

10. Spanish team Cristiano Ronaldo scored his fourth La Liga hat-trick against way back in 2011! (10)

11. Name of Paul Pogba's famous celebration! (3)

12. Name of small-sided indoor footy that Rodrygo Goes played as a kid! (6)

14. Mega boot brand that Liverpool and Egypt's Mo Salah wears! (6)

18. Number of Champions League titles Franck Ribery has won! (3)

THE NICKNAME GAME!

Have a go at matching the mind-blowing trick machines to their awesome nicknames!

 **Lionel Messi** ◈ 1

 **Paulo Dybala** ◈ 2

 **Ricardo Quaresma** ◈ 3

 **Franck Ribery** ◈ 4

 **Angel Di Maria** ◈ 5

 **Willian** ◈ 6

◈ A **Beckham**

◈ B **Noodle**

◈ C **The Flea**

◈ D **Ferrari**

◈ E **The Jewel**

◈ F **Harry Potter**

 **Oussama Assaidi**

 **Dimitri Payet**

 **Hatem Ben Arfa**

 **Aiden McGeady**

ODD ONE OUT!

 **Julian Draxler**

Which of these top-quality dribblers hasn't played for a Premier League team?

Nani

ANSWER ON P6

FIFA SKILLS

Learn to bust out some jaw-dropping tricks while juggling on FIFA!

JUGGLING ★

First things first, get the ball up into the air by juggling with your player!

HOLD: L2/LT /

TAP: R1/RB /

AROUND THE WORLD ★★★★★

Throw in an extra piece of flair with this mind-blowing 5-star trick!

ROTATE: R Stick Up, Right, Down, Left   **OR** R Stick Down, Left, Up, Right

TOUZANI AROUND THE WORLD ★★★★★

Go further with mad showboating!

ROTATE: R Stick Up, Right, Down Left

FLICK: R Stick Up

IN-AIR ELASTICO ★★★★★

Only the best skillers can manage this piece of skill!

FLICK: R Stick Right, R Stick Left

OR FLICK: R Stick Left, R Stick Right

SOMBRERO FLICK ★★★★★

Defenders won't know where the ball is at if you bust out this sick skill!

HOLD: L Stick Down

3

RIYAD MAHREZ

TOP SKILL!
THE STEPOVER!

Club: Man. City
Country: Algeria
DOB: 21/02/91

Mahrez has said before that his all-time favourite skill is the stepover, but we've seen the winger perform all sorts of five-star tricks, including the Elastico and Turn and Spin! His dribbling is incredible, too – the ball just sticks to his left boot like it's got Super Glue on it!

DID YOU KNOW?

THE SKILLER WAS APPROACHED BY PSG AT 19, BUT DECIDED TO DEVELOP HIS GAME WITH LIGUE 2 SIDE LE HAVRE INSTEAD!

CONFIDENCE
95

DRIBBLING
90

TRICKS
95

AGILITY
93

WEAK FOOT
88

2
DOUGLAS COSTA

JUVENTUS

Club: *Juventus*
Country: *Brazil*
DOB: *14/09/90*

You'll catch Costa pulling off five-star flicks in warm-ups – but he doesn't have any issue busting them out during games either! He's one of a handful of stars that MATCH has seen perform a rainbow flick in a match – his one from 2016 was just out of this world!

DID YOU KNOW?

THE BRAZILIAN KING COMPLETED 106 DRIBBLES ON LOAN AT JUVENTUS LAST SEASON – MORE THAN ANY OTHER SERIE A PLAYER. WOW!

CONFIDENCE
100

DRIBBLING
90

TRICKS
100

AGILITY
95

WEAK FOOT
80

1

NEYMAR

Club: PSG
Country: Brazil
DOB: 5/02/92

The Triple Elastico, Fake Rabona and Sombrero – all of the hardest tricks you can imagine – Neymar has pulled them off in a match! His hunger to wow fans with new tricks – like his outrageous back touch and rainbow flick from last season – make him easily MATCH's No.1 skiller on the planet!

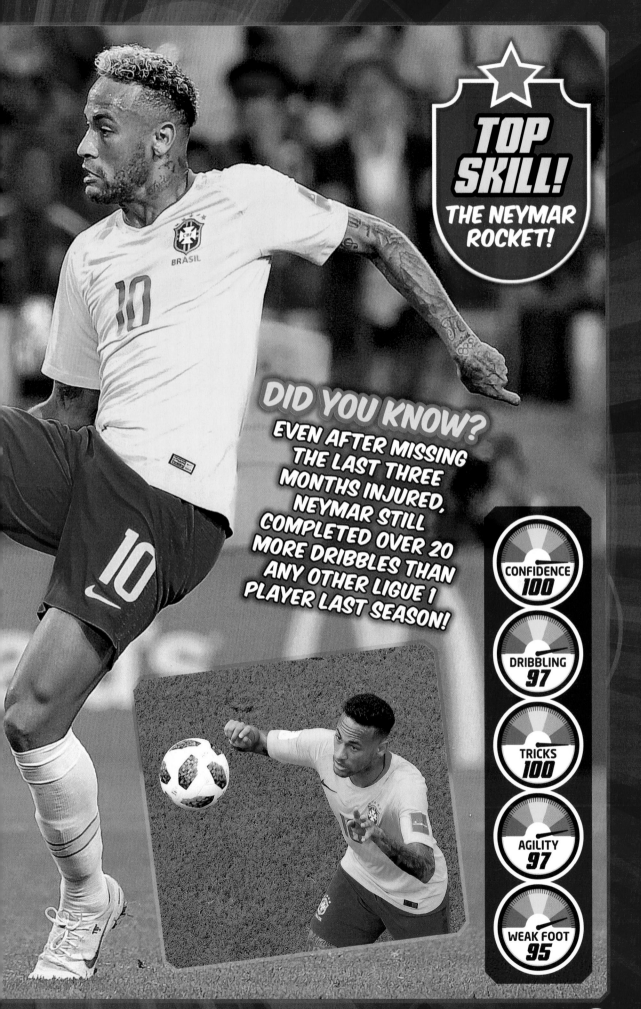

TOP SKILL!
THE NEYMAR ROCKET!

DID YOU KNOW?
EVEN AFTER MISSING THE LAST THREE MONTHS INJURED, NEYMAR STILL COMPLETED OVER 20 MORE DRIBBLES THAN ANY OTHER LIGUE 1 PLAYER LAST SEASON!

CONFIDENCE
100

DRIBBLING
97

TRICKS
100

AGILITY
97

WEAK FOOT
95

TOP 50... STAT ATTACK!

Player/Club	Dribbles
Lionel Messi *Barcelona*	185
Eden Hazard *Chelsea*	165
Neymar *PSG*	142
Wilfried Zaha *Crystal Palace*	119
David Neres *Ajax*	114
Douglas Costa *Juventus*	106
Paulo Dybala *Juventus*	93
Philippe Coutinho *Barcelona*	85
Leroy Sane *Man. City*	85
Alexis Sanchez *Man. United*	84

You've seen our Top 50 Skillers countdown, now check out the wicked tricksters by club, country, age and more!

11

An epic 11 of the 50 sick skill kings have won the Champions League!

TOP 50 BY...
CLUB!

Club	No. of Players
Bayern Munich	4
Juventus	4
PSG	4
Barcelona	3
Man. City	3
Chelsea	2
Liverpool	2
Man. United	2
Real Madrid	2
Ajax	1
Aston Villa	1
Atletico Madrid	1
Besiktas	1
Celta Vigo	1
Crystal Palace	1
Everton	1
FC Twente	1
Flamengo	1
Marseille	1
Montreal Impact	1
Napoli	1
Porto	1
Roma	1
Santos	1
Schalke	1
Shakhtar Donetsk	1
Southampton	1
Sporting	1
Sunderland	1
Tottenham	1
Vitesse	1
West Ham	1

100+

Only four of the tricksters had won over 100 caps for their country before World Cup 2018 – Sanchez, Messi, Ronaldo and Nani!

TOP 50 BY...
BOOTS!

Boots	No. of Players
Nike Mercurial	28
adidas X	10
adidas Nemeziz	6
adidas Predator	3
Nike Hypervenom	2
Puma One	1

TOP 50 BY...
LEAGUE!

League	No. of Players
Premier League	14
La Liga	7
Serie A	6
Bundesliga	5
Ligue 1	5
Eredivisie	3
Primeira Liga	2
Brazilian Serie A	2
Championship	1
League One	1
MLS	1
Turkish Super Lig	1
Ukrainian Premier League	1

TOP 10 BY...
AGE – YOUNGEST

Player	Age
Rodrygo	17
Kylian Mbappe	19
Amine Harit	21
Ousmane Dembele	21
Richarlison	21
Gabriel Jesus	21
David Neres	21
Charly Musonda	21
Kingsley Coman	22
Dele Alli	22

83%

Of all the players that completed over 60 league dribbles in 2017-18, Eden Hazard had the best success rate!

Dimitri Payet made more league key passes – ones that led to a shot at goal from a team-mate – than any other hero on our list in 2017-18. Ledge!

121

TOP 10 BY...
AGE – OLDEST

Player	Age
Franck Ribery	35
Ricardo Quaresma	34
Ignacio Piatti	33
Cristiano Ronaldo	33
Aiden McGeady	32
Nani	31
Hatem Ben Arfa	31
Dimitri Payet	31
Lionel Messi	31
Angel Di Maria	30

TOP 50 BY...
COUNTRY!

Country	No. of Players
Brazil	11
France	7
Argentina	4
Portugal	4
Morocco	3
Belgium	2
Colombia	2
Germany	2
Italy	2
Spain	2
Ukraine	2
Algeria	1
Cameroon	1
Chile	1
DR Congo	1
Egypt	1
England	1
Ivory Coast	1
Norway	1
Republic Of Ireland	1

80+

No player on the list has scored more international goals than CR7. Legend!

All ages correct up to the start of the 2018-19 season.

MATCH! ACADEMY
Play like the stars!

MOHAMED SALAH
THE HOOK TURN!

TIP 1: GAME USE

You can use this awesome 1 v 1 move anywhere in the attacking third of the pitch - just like Liverpool and Egypt goal king Mo Salah! Make sure to keep the ball on your furthest foot from the defender and use your upper body to protect it. Sweet!

THIS SKILL HELPS YOU...

Change direction and shield the ball! ✓

Create more goal chances! ✓

Dominate your opponent in 1 v 1 situations! ✓

TIP 2: DEFENDER POSITION

Use the Hook Turn 1 v 1 move when you have a defender blocking you right in front or to the side. Reds legend Salah does it all the time in the Prem to create an opportunity to play a sick killer pass or make space for a shot with his deadly left foot!

Turn over now to book your FREE Coerver® Performance Academy training session!

TRAINING GROUND!

Now practise doing the Hook Turn!

STEP 1

Push the ball forward with your right foot.

STEP 2

With the same foot, fake to strike the ball and hook it back behind your standing leg.

STEP 3

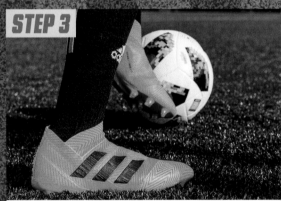

Turn 180 degrees and accelerate away from your marker using your left foot! Repeat using your left foot to hook and right foot to take away.

NOW WATCH EPIC VIDEOS!

Learn how to do loads of top tricks by visiting the MATCH Academy section on our website!

www.matchfootball.co.uk

COMPETITION

WORDFIT

Fit the wicked tricksters who didn't quite make our Top 50 list into this giant grid!

Botaka	Ilsinho	Pereira
Carrillo	Kishna	Perisic
Cengiz	Kluivert	Pulisic
Chanturia	Lamela	Rakhale
Depay	Manuel	Robben
Elton	Mastour	Shikabala
Fernandez	Maxim	Taarabt
Flores	Oberlin	Talisca
Giuliano	Paqueta	Villanueva
Ibrahimovic	Pavon	Ziyech

5 QUESTIONS ON...
RIYAD MAHREZ

1 Which of Europe's big five leagues did the Man. City trickster play in first?

2 How old was the Algeria ace when he joined Leicester back in 2014?

3 What year was he crowned African Footballer Of The Year – 2015 or 2016?

4 Has he made more or less than 30 senior appearances for his country?

5 True or False? The mind-blowing trick king was actually born in France!

SPOT THE BALL!

Mark where you think the ball is in this pic with sick skiller Pogba!

ANSWERS ON P60

Face In The Crowd P21

Brainbuster P20

1. False; 2. England;
3. 2013; 4. Man. United;
5. Lille; 6. Fewer than ten;
7. DR Congo; 8. Barcelona;
9. Nike; 10. Left footed.

Wordsearch P30

Footy Mis-Match P31

Crossword P44

The Nickname Game P45

Messi – The Flea;
Dybala – The Jewel;
Quaresma – Harry Potter;
Ribery – Ferrari;
Di Maria – Noodle;
Willian – Beckham.

Odd One Out P45

Julian Draxler.

Riyad Mahrez Quiz P59

1. Ligue 1;
2. 22 years old;

3. 2016;
4. More than 30;
5. True.

Spot The Ball P59

F2.

Wordfit P58